# the world that destroyed the world

## *a poem*

Sean::Adrian::Brijbasi

Published simultaneously in the United States and Great Britain in 2019
by Pretend Genius
Copyright © Sean::Adrian::Brijbasi

This book is copyright under the Berne Convention
No reproduction without permission
All rights reserved

ISBN: 978-0-9995277-8-8

other books by Sean::Adrian::Brijbasi

One Note Symphonies
*for Emma*

Still Life in Motion
*for those who play*
*Marius and Andréus*

The Unknowed Things
*for Julius*

The Dictionary of Coincidences, Volume i
*for Emma*

S{E}AN?
*for EM{M}A+*

E{M}MA+ the ghost orchids
*for Emma*

darling two hearts
*for E{M}MA+ the ghost orchids*

Stories for Nadira
*for Adrian, Andréus, Elijah, Helena, Julius, Marius,*
*Nadira*

Play Championship World-Class
Tennis with Bjorn McEnroe
*for Adrian, Andréus, Elijah, Helena, Julius, Marius,*
*Nadira*

*for*

*Adrian*

*Andreus*

*Elijah*

*Helena*

*Julius*

*Marius*

*Nadira*

| | |
|---|---|
| prologue | i |
| chapter 1 | 1 |

"I am a forest, and a night of dark trees: but who is not afraid of my darkness, will find banks full of roses under my cypresses."

*--F.N.*

## prologue

The train stopped and I saw the woman and man walking on the road below—she a few feet in front of him, carrying a book she read from as she took little steps in the new-fallen snow, he listening to music on his headphones while looking up to the cloudy sky, seemingly unaware of any obstacles he might stumble upon along his path.

They appeared to come from different worlds whose storylines would only intersect under the strangest of circumstances. Perhaps they were a hallucination from a fairytale in which the characters of different fairytales appeared randomly in the world I lived in (such is the life of fairytale characters) and found each other because there were no other fairytale characters to find.

Or perhaps they were two vampires from different ancient centuries pulled from their own time by an unseen cosmic force to the present where they held on to each other in the corner of a room of eternal light only able to survive because of the slit of a shadow cast by the window frame and the exchange of a few drops of blood for the occasional midnight nibble.

The woman's hair trailed behind her in the wind and (in my mind's nose) I smelled the faintest aroma of ginger blossoms in the train cabin, which returned my senses to the moment in which I lived, so that I saw the woman and the man for what they really were: two people.

The man caught up to the woman and they walked beside each other, disappearing from my view (her hair reaching out behind her as if it wanted me to reach out in return), leaving only the stepped-upon snow as evocation, if not evidence, that what I saw was real and therefore really happened.

I was of two minds: mind 1) the woman and the man knew each other (intimately) because they walked beside each other without speaking; mind 2) the woman and the man didn't know each other (intimately)—two opposite minds—but had perhaps felt inside themselves the inklings of a mutual attraction and didn't want to part company until one of them decided that she or he didn't have the courage to say whatever it was that was on her or his mind.

I hope they did have the courage (I give it to them if they don't) and said to each other "I like you" and "I like you too"— words only they could hear despite being muted by the hustle and bustle of life around them (the car engines, the delivery men shouting across the street, the station bell ringing the train's departure)—and moved closer together to touch shoulders and the backs of each other's hands (even though the man wore mittens and didn't have the courage—I can only give so much—to take them off).

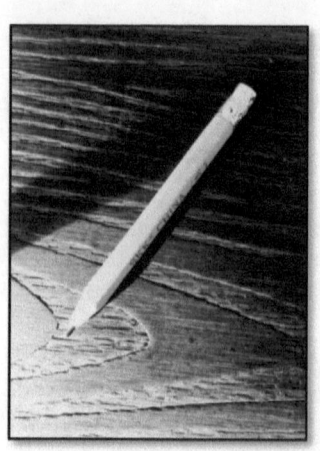

# chapter 1

M. limped down the stairs from the train station to the road where the taxi drivers parked their taxis to wait for late night travelers.  M. was a late night traveler and thought about cuddling up with Jolene in a nook near the station newspaper and assorted goods shop because he didn't have anywhere else to cuddle up.  But he saw the bronze[1] poking at an old man lying on the floor against a well-kept looking vending machine and decided to cuddle up elsewhere.  He could barely make out the snacks behind the vending machine glass and the juices in his stomach churned loudly enough for him to hear but no one else.

He had some money for a taxi and he'd ask the taxi driver if there was a clean, cheap

---
[1] Police

place he could stay for the night. Tomorrow he'd be meeting friends. Or that was the plan. They weren't plans per se and they weren't friends per se. He met them (a sister, a brother, and brother's girlfriend) a couple of weeks before and hundreds of miles away at the little train station in Fristad.

They had spent the day together, walking from park to park, sitting on park benches, picnicking on freshly-cut park grass, before going their separate ways. The girlfriend told him that if he was ever passing through the 6 Cities (down in the lower continent) he could get in touch (she scribbled her address on a piece of paper) and she (and the boyfriend he supposed) would show him all the places tourists missed when they visited. It was a sentiment M. shared with other travelers and he understood the invitation was probably more the consequence of good manners than good intentions because that's just how some travelers said good-bye. He had said good-bye in the same way on many occasions although he didn't have a city to call home.

He got along peachy with the girlfriend (maybe too peachy) but not too peachy with the sister (prickly pearish) who never spoke to him and barely ever looked at him. The boyfriend was so-so (turnipy) who didn't notice the small things that his girlfriend noticed (the woman sleeping on the park bench beneath the oak tree, the sun shining on her feet, her head resting on what looked like the carapace of a semi-giant red-footed tortoise).

But the hour was late and he would find his new friends (per se) the next day. If he found them—great. If not—oh well. "Great and oh well" was how he lived his life.

It was a dark night and the darkest part of the night lingered around the taxis like a fog. It was a darkness that made him want to drop down right where he stood and fall asleep as a door was being closed to block out the last photon bursts of light reaching his pupils or (even better) as he was being buried so he could feel the insect-like texture of dirt on his face as his eyes became too heavy to keep open (in the first instance he could hear the door hinges creaking and in the second the shovel stabbing the soft earth). The less dark part of the night was off in the distance somewhere. That's where he was headed.

He looked through the passenger-side window of the taxi (the first three letters of the Latin alphabet rendered in lower-case on the passenger door, the bulbous curvature of the roof bringing to mind the painting "Pregnant Woman in Repose" by American impressionist Helen Willis) and tapped on the slightly tinted glass. The taxi driver looked him over before she unlocked the doors. He settled into the backseat. She asked him where he wanted to go. He said he didn't know.

"Do you know a place? I've never been here before."

"There are a few", she said. "I can take you to one of them. Don't know if it'll have room for you and then I'd have to drive you somewhere else and that'd cost you more money."

M. could get more money in the morning but he didn't have enough money for two taxi rides and a place to stay. He'd just have to take a chance. The night was always a dice roll to him. There were a million things he could choose to do and a million-and-one things he could choose not to do but he learned the hard way (like those Japanese Ikebana lessons) that he never had control of the night. He made his plans, he showered, he ironed his favorite shirt, and while he tied the laces on his favorite pair of shoes, he pictured how the night would start, how the night would end, and everything in between. But he never knew (he couldn't even say "anything") because at night the perfectly ordinary could lead to the inexplicable.

The day was different. The day had structure—scaffolding to keep him safe. A framework in which what he did (unless he did something extraordinary—which he never did) had little effect on what happened to him. He'd still end up at home (or someplace) tired of life but wanting more. And yet he felt like a liminal creature during the day, despite the day's structure, unsure of who he was and what he was becoming. At night, surrounded by the nebulousness around him, he felt that his being had a crust at least, regardless of the existence of any fruit or cream filling. The crust was the tastiest part anyway, the part that night people liked to chew up, leaving anyone who did have any fruit or cream filling as a mass of goo with nothing holding them together. He sometimes thought that was better than not being chewed up at all but he wasn't sure which he preferred (fruit or cream). And yet, if all twenty-four hours of the day were included, he felt (overall) like a liminal creature.

The taxi driver turned up the radio volume. M.'s gaze lingered on her hand and fingers and he thought about Clementine and deduced in the manner he was taught by Clementine that the taxi driver bit her fingernails. He looked up to the rear-view mirror to spy her forehead and caught a glimpse of her eyes on the way there. She had the smoothest forehead he had seen in a long time. If he had spent more time with Clementine he might have understood what the smoothness meant. He and Clementine met under calamitous circumstances but even she would agree they shared a rapport that belied the perceived social strata each occupied. His backpack (Jolene) leaned against him like a tired friend. The taxi driver turned the radio volume down as she spoke.

"It's cold tonight", she said.

M. didn't think it was cold at all. In fact, as far as habitable temperatures went, he thought it was in the comfortable range for human beings. He imagined the conversation.

*--No, it's not cold at all.*

*--It is.*

*--It's not.*

"A little", he said.

She turned the radio volume up again. The song playing on the radio reminded him of a song he had heard before but didn't know the words to. He leaned his head against the backseat head-rest, looking through the window—at all the slumbering buildings and the trees here and there that swayed them to their slumbering—and remembered the dream he had on his short trip to the 6 Cities. The dreams he had on trains were always too ripe as if too much time had passed in between train rides so that he couldn't pluck the perfect dream from the dream tree that grew inside his head. Instead the dreams became too juicy, past their perfect-plucking age, and fell on him as he walked by, breaking apart on his face—striking the nose first (he was always looking up, to the sky in general, to the clouds or stars or birds in particular) so that the dream juices splattered all over him, making his body sticky, especially his arms, because for reasons he didn't understand he never wore long sleeves in his dreams. His dreams in buildings and non-moving objects were never ripe enough. Barely developed from the seed. His dreams on boats were always the perfect balance of real-life and dream substances.

He was at the yearly family summer get-together at his parent's house when, through the living room window, he spied his older brother standing on the walkway leading to the house, looking up at the tall oak tree they climbed when they were young. The sun shone through the branches and leaves of the tree, reaching the ground in front of his brother's feet, as if a messenger had arrived after a long journey and bowed before him. M. opened the door and asked his brother if he wanted to come inside but his brother said no ("nah") in that difficult-to-place drawl he had picked up from somewhere on his travels and about which M. had perhaps remarked one too many times ("you didn't always talk like that"). M. closed the door. He expected to hear the doorbell ring and when he didn't he peeked through the window to see that his brother was gone. Maybe he knocked instead and no one heard him. Maybe the message was just that important.

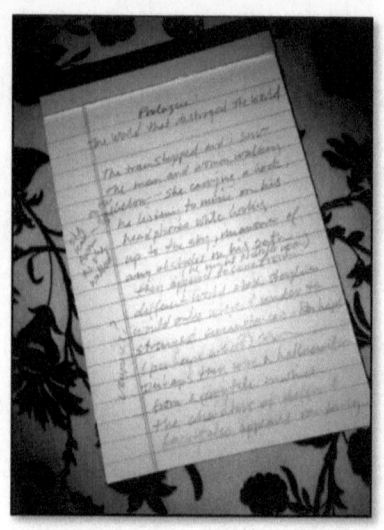

The dream was an exact replica of the real-life occurrence and depicted in perfect detail (down to the short sleeves that M. wore) the last time he saw his brother. In fact, it didn't seem like a dream at all but something that happened in real life that happened again, so that he felt (in essence) he was remembering his memory about that day and not (as it first seemed) the dream about the memory of that day. He didn't understand why his brother disappeared or why he never returned. For years after his brother's disappearance M. sat alone on sofas or any furniture-like object (railings, highway traffic barriers, patio retaining walls) that could seat more than one person, leaving a space for his brother, as if his brother would walk in from the imaginary land of nowhere and sit down beside him. His girlfriends never understood (he wanted to tell them but never told them the origin of his sitting behavior) and often broke up with him because they didn't feel the intimacy from him that any normal girlfriend might expect.

M. liked to think (when he thought about it) that if his brother was dead that he died on M.'s birthday because it made him feel like he and his brother were twin stars forever orbiting each other while the world (which included the universe in M.'s mind) fell apart (or not) around them. And if not twin stars then it was simply that his brother had gone away for a while and that he would see him again one day. But he didn't like to think about it at all (ever) because even the faintest shadow of the thought or the faintest shadows of any thoughts related to the faintest shadow of the main thought prevented him from taking the smallest step on any one of the paths that offered an escape from the thick forest of darkness around him.

He felt the ache in his foot again and stretched his leg sideways behind the driver's seat, careful not to kick the seat and distract the driver from her mental navigations. He had gotten his foot stuck in the train tracks at the Amsterdam train station and suffered severe bruising in his toes and upper foot area as the foot was being extracted. Since then he walked with a limp as his foot healed (slowly, to ensure that all the connective tissues between the skin and bone reconnected properly). It was Clementine who unstuck his foot and saved him although she made it clear to him that the train wouldn't have pushed into the station until she got his foot unstuck so he wasn't in any real danger and therefore didn't need saving in the way that someone who was in real danger needed saving.

M. wasn't convinced. She had saved him. He felt that he and Clementine met at the only inn in the middle of a desolate countryside in which a torch had to be lit to let the inn-keepers—who lived in a house miles down the road—know (they trained their dog to bark at fire) that their inn-keeping services were required.

It would take an hour or two for the inn-keepers to get themselves ready in the middle of that steamy night and gather whatever supplies they needed to feed and house M. and Clementine and then carry those supplies to the inn by a wagon pulled by their old, trusty horse.

In the meantime, M. and Clementine would poke around the inn and find, pick up, and put back small objects left behind by other travelers: small ceramic elephant, working compass, monocle with string, wooden knife for butter and margarine, black-and-white photograph of woman leaning out of downtown apartment window, small metal bowl containing hair barrette, assorted coins from foreign lands (America, Thailand, Romania).

When the inn-keepers arrived, their dog would bark at M. and Clementine as the two moved closer together. M. felt this at the very moment Clementine yanked his foot from the tracks and not a moment after or days after and he thought that the entire world (which included the universe) stopped whatever it was doing to catch that fleeting moment before returning to its usual spiraling and gravitational handiwork.

The city was quiet. Traffic lights blinked. Street lights flickered. The taxi driver moved her foot from the accelerator to the brake, bringing the taxi to a smooth stop, in front of a building with two architectural features that M. recognized from his readings: a portico at the entrance and, on either side of the portico, support beams sculpted into the shape of Pallas Athena on the left and Aphrodite on the right (he conjectured).

"This is the place", she said.

M. knew a thing or two about architecture because it was the subject he and his brother talked about when they apologized to each other after they argued (or wronged each other in some way)—a subject mixed into their already awkward apologies like a spoonful of coffee grinds in a cup of warm, medicinal tea, or perhaps more like the slow removal of a sticky plaster that intensified the fraternal tenderness of the nerves beneath. They didn't have to apologize often but when they did the conversation surrounding the apology could go on for hours. M. read about architecture (just in case) because he felt that the conversations surrounding their apologies shouldn't be the same—the apologies wouldn't feel sincere. One morning he forgot to go to work because he and his brother apologized to each other while discussing the constructivist period of Le Corbusier. When his brother found out that he had kept M. from going to work, he called M. again to apologize, at which time he apologized (and M. accepted apology), while discussing the narrower subject of Le Corbusier's *Chapelle Notre Dame du Haut in Ronchamp*.

M. eventually did go to work and continued to do so for several years until his brother disappeared (and didn't return) at which time he vowed he would never go to work again. He thought he could have made a name for himself in his chosen industry (plastics) if he had continued and then after a long retirement devoted to attracting hummingbirds or growing fruits and vegetables, rest honorably (perhaps even nobly) in his black suit, white shirt, and black tie, arms crossed over his chest—his favorite book (Introduction to Greek Architecture by Thelma Evans) looking as if it was—indeed—simply tucked beneath the intersection of his stiffened wrists, unable to hear the sobbing of those who loved him and the polite voices of those who only liked him. He took some money from his pocket and handed it to the taxi driver. As she turned he thought he saw a faint line on her forehead.

"I'll wait for you", she said.

"Thank you", he said.

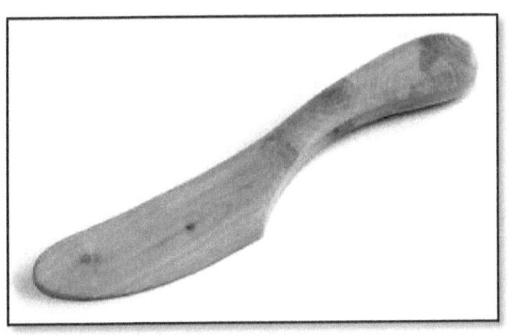

He stepped out of the taxi (Jolene slung over his shoulder) and stood in front of the portico. He observed the words "The Tenth Portal" carved into the concrete tympanum—degraded over time but still legible at night or on a dark day if the artificial lights from the nearby street lamps fell on each letter at just the right angle (therefore the need for observation). It looked like the entrance to a place where one might find the succulent core of existence or (perhaps) the mouthwatering quintessence of being—if one were looking.

He opened the door. Nobody—only a desk with a bell on it and across from the desk, between two windows, a wooden bench that had scratched the wooden floor as it slid back and forth from the weight and motion of weary travelers. He rang the bell. *Ping.* No one. He rang again (a double ring). *Ping ping.* Still no one. He turned the doorknob on the door to the stairway but it was locked. He pushed the elevator button. The elevator door opened and for a moment (even less) he thought about getting into the elevator and stopping at each floor. But the dispatch with which the elevator door opened gave him the sense that he was being lured into the mouth of a large, unknowable organism that would swallow him whole. He waited until the elevator door closed before he took a step back.

Perhaps there were giant amoeba-like affairs going on above him but he had nowhere else to stay. He thought he could sleep on the wooden bench. No. He wouldn't sleep. He would wait. He would wait and in the act of waiting he would fall asleep. If someone appeared they would wake him (nudge him gently) and he would say he was waiting because he wanted a room for the night. If no one appeared then he would sleep. Yes, he would sleep. He thought that if he hadn't already understood waiting (understood it deeply) he would have felt that he had stumbled upon the key (or one of the keys) of his life: waiting, and while waiting, doing something or even doing nothing. He went back outside and told the taxi driver that he would wait inside.

"There's no one there now", he said. "I think I'll just wait inside."

"Stay warm", the taxi driver said.

He imagined the conversation.

*--But it's not cold.*

*--It is.*

"You too", he said.

As she drove the taxi in reverse it seemed to him that their gazes locked for longer than usual and that she was being pulled into an ever-narrowing circle of darkness from which she could only be freed by the muscle power of his eyes and a minute or two of undistracted mental concentration (easily broken by the sound of her voice).

"Just let me go", he heard her say from across the road and through the metal and glass of her taxi. "From inside here as if inside night and every night I can hear the machinations of people who tune themselves in fits of tightening and loosening of this or that thought or gesture or expression to make themselves ready for the performance they will play with other people, some tuned and some un-tuned, to send out into the universe and across the arc of the world the clamor and discord of human existence but which is, almost inexplicably, from time to time, penetrated by the strains of people whose thoughts or gestures or expressions are brought into harmony by some goddess or god of chance."

Then she turned her head to see where she was going and drove to the intersection. M. went back into the building. He placed Jolene on one end of the bench and lay on his back, resting his head on the softest part of her. He turned on his right side—his favorite sleeping position—and looked at the bell on the front desk. It was shiny and he could see the reflection of the surrounding environment in the bell's polished, sloping dome: the elevator door and the wall around it, the door to the stairway and the wall around it, the entrance/exit door with the exit sign above and the wall around it, the windows on either side of M. and Jolene lying on the wooden bench and the wall around it (them), and the ceiling and the lumen-or-two-too-bright ceiling bulb that seemed to leak radiance from a more posh neighborhood of provincial chairs, French armoires, and coffee tables with glass table tops, each held up by one of the Muses (or Furies or Fates) sculpted in marble, and in which someone like him or someone not at all like him recounted tales of derring-do to enchanted demoiselles and chevaliers too young to have tales of derring-do of their own to recount. Or sometimes he talked about his new favorite song (*The Trees They Grow So*

*Tall*) while occasionally playing his galoubet (pipe and tambourine), tapping his foot to keep the time. He imagined the conversation he would have with the girlfriend the next day.

*--Do you remember the woman sleeping in the park?*

*--I do.*

*--She was sleeping really well.*

*--She was. She was sleeping so well that the tree drooped around her like it was sleeping too.*

*--She was sleeping so well that the roots that we couldn't see under the tree used the dirt around them as pillows and rested for the first time in hundreds of years.*

*--They couldn't sleep because of all the foot stomping above.*

*--Do you think anyone else noticed her?*

*--Foot stomping reminds me of dancing.*

He heard the sound of pitter-pattering against the window. A light rain fell.

*--Was it in remember?*

*--Remember is a long month.*

*--What month?*

He fell asleep and dreamed that he lived in a time before the first sadness, before the first sickness, before the first death. He wasn't a caveman in his dream. He was just as he was in modern times. He wore the same clothes and spoke the same language and walked the raw earth for the short amount of time that it existed before the first of anything. Even the sky was raw— discolored with the lightest shade of blood from its difficult birth. The water in the streams and rivers. Raw. The trees on the land. Raw. The wind in the air. Raw.

"Wake up", the man said.

M. opened his eyes and sat upright. He pulled Jolene close to his leg (his mind still in a haze) and felt that if he stood up he would tip over and fall back into his dream—an unearthly place where he was uncertain of what he would do to the strange man (who he might have seen—rightly or wrongly—as the personification of the peculiar and growing idea of *adversary* in his brain) with the ethos of such a world permeating every part of his being.

"You can't stay here", the man said.

"I was waiting and fell asleep. I just want a room for the night", M. said.

"No rooms. No one is staying here tonight", the man said.

"But the bell is working", M. said.

"You have to go somewhere else", the man said.

M. picked up Jolene and walked outside. He watched the man turn the lock on the door and draw the curtain closed as he stood on the proscenium of that concrete and glass stage, his back to the audience, no script, no director, and no play in which to play himself or perform as someone else.

Light drops of rain fell on his face. A puddle of water by his feet reflected the portico and the dark night sky around him.

He didn't know how long he had been sleeping (the warmth from his sleep still emanated from his body) but he saw the taxi driver parked at the intersection. He limped across the road.

"What happened?" she asked.

"They don't have any rooms", he said.

"You must be freezing", she said. "Get in."

"I don't know where else to go", he said.

He thought he should have taken the elevator from floor to floor. He could have slept in the hallway, maybe on the highest floor. The very top. No one would have seen him until morning. He'd take the stairs all the way down unnoticed. Even with his tender foot—hopping on his strong foot—descending step by step, resting on every third or fourth floor, reaching the bottom, then pausing to catch his breath before crossing the threshold (the words "filled with possibility" etched on the pediment above) into the new world (which included the universe) on the other side.

As the taxi pulled away M. saw a light go on in one of the rooms on the top floor of the building. A woman and a man stood at the window. The man took off his shirt and tossed it on the bed. The woman brushed her hair, the length of which covered her shoulders and breasts. A puff of smoke drifted through the opening and then one more into that space where the light from inside and the darkness from outside mingled as if at a gathering of weary soldiers on hiatus from the eternal battle they waged. The man pulled down the window with both hands to close it. The woman got in bed—her uncovered back momentarily visible as she turned (a landscape where—M. imagined—the scent of jasmine picked from the fields of faraway kingdoms enchanted the apple and pear traders and the children who hid beneath their carts to steal from them) and pulled the blanket over her body. The man put out his cigarette on the bedside table and lay down on top of the blanket next to her. The room went dark.

It was as if M. had been staring at a photograph that he held up by a window through which the moon in the vast darkness of night reflected barely enough sun from across the void to make the woman and man in the photograph visible to him before he placed it on his desk and into the smaller darkness of his room though still vast enough to obscure the woman and man in the photograph, the photograph itself, and the hand that placed it there.

The feeling of the present warm night and the memory of the feeling from a past warm night (with Clementine) merged in his body (where he couldn't tell) and he was overcome with a feeling of "the sad enchantment of life". On the day leading up to the warm night he and Clementine ate noodles at a small Chinese diner (making little hearts out of black paper napkins while they waited), watched boats sail up and down the city canal, lay on the grass at Hanami Park looking up at clouds drift across the blue sky (he remembered wondering how he could go on); and then the warm night and watching Clementine sleep beside him on the floor of the small, desolate train station as they waited for their trains, her train going in one direction, his going in another. He had hoped she would stay awake because while she was sleeping she was somewhere else and no longer with him.

A woman's voice announced the next train's arrival and M. thought about the message his brother might have gotten the last time he saw him. It was a mental message from deep inside his brother's being that had been written and rewritten hundreds of times until it finally got through to him because everything (everything—the time of day, the temperature, the sun shining through the trees, the memory of M.'s voice he had just heard, the latitude and longitude of the position of his body outside their parent's house, the velocity of the breeze that glanced his face as it passed by him—everything) aligned perfectly to make the message finally understandable to him (both the meaning and the urgent need to reply).

M. wanted to believe that he had also received a message (just like his brother)—Clementine sleeping beside him (even in the din he could hear her breathing), the woman's voice around him, the angle of his right leg as he sat on the station floor, the velocity of the breeze from the incoming train on his face—but nothing aligned perfectly to make the message understandable.

Drops of rain fell on the front windshield of the taxi and slid slowly down the glass, the shadows of which appeared as black dots on the dashboard, like insects crawling towards the taxi's grey dashboard horizon. Some reached their destination while others were erased from their already brief existence with a single pass of the windshield wiper. M. felt no shame remembering the time he spent with

Clementine at the train station. But the memory was still new. With older memories, even good ones, he always felt a pang of shame. Not because he had done anything to be ashamed of but because it became clear to him (years later and sometimes only months later) that he didn't know who he was and was only pretending to be someone he wasn't so that he always had an urge to interrupt his memories—as his present self—to say to anyone else in those memories: "I'm sorry but this isn't really me".

He settled into the backseat again, closed his eyes, and imagined himself standing in the doorway on the other side of the apartment building they had just left while the taxi driver (no longer with her taxi) sat on a swing in the playground, surrounded by apartment buildings, from through the window of one, the mother and father of a girl who was too weak with fever to go to school (or even raise her head) looked down and quietly hoped tomorrow would be a better day. The taxi driver stood up from the swing and walked to her taxi. M. moved from the dim light underneath the doorway and followed her.

They were on their way to the Woodleworth discount goods shop. The taxi driver had made the decision to go to the shop when she thought (and certainly he thought) they would never see each other again. The Woodleworth was a neighborhood institution that opened in the early 21st century. "Open Later Than Any Other Shop In The World" were the words engraved on its front door though that wasn't always the case. It used to close at six o'clock on the dot so that the owner

(Mrs. Woodleworth) and her husband (Mr. Woodleworth) could have dinner together and while away the night until, one freezing winter morning as Mrs. Woodleworth walked towards the entrance of her shop to open the door and make preparations for another day of pleasing her loyal customers, she found a man (a traveler passing through the city it came to be known) frozen to death beneath the large shop window not more than three feet from the door itself. There was no existential crisis to be had about the incident ("how many can one have in a lifetime?" she was heard saying) but a few days later, after all the city investigations (both procedural and philosophical), when Mrs. Woodleworth slowly pulled open the door to the shop again it was as if the eyelid of a human being in perpetual sleep opened so that the apparatus of vision that lay behind the eyelid would take in all that it could take in for as long as it could so that anyone who wanted to be taken in would be taken in without regard to appearance, bouquet, or circumstance.

"They have food in there too", the taxi driver said. "Cans and cans of food. You can come with me."

"Are you sure the shop is opened?" he asked.

"It never closes", she said.

He walked behind her through the shop door and saw a young man sitting at the cash register reading a book. The taxi driver pointed to the shelf where the cans of food were located and headed down another aisle. M. read the labels on the different cans of food, most of which contained meat, vegetables, and rice. As he read about the nutritional value on a can of green beans he heard voices and peeked around the shelf to see who was speaking: two women (he could only see their backs) and, furthermore, he thought he recognized the voice of the woman who was speaking. When she turned her head to look at the other woman, he saw that she was the girlfriend (peachy) he met in Fristad—the one who noticed things that others didn't notice (the woman sleeping on the park bench beneath the oak tree, the sun shining on her feet, her head resting on what looked like the carapace of a semi-giant red-footed tortoise). The woman she was talking to was her sister (prickly pearish) who never spoke to him and barely ever looked at him.

He picked up a can of food (the very same green beans) from the shelf and walked towards the cash register. He adjusted Jolene on his shoulder and, as he did, the can of green beans slipped out of his hand and clanged against the linoleum floor. The two women turned around (the man at the register looked up). The girlfriend looked at him and he looked at her. He waited for that moment of mutual recognition between them but the moment never came and the girlfriend turned back around to continue speaking to the man at the register. The sister smiled at him. Or he thought she smiled. Whatever expression she had on her face was different from the first time they met when she barely looked at him.

He picked up the can, took a few more steps to the register, and stood behind the two women. The sister glanced at him every few seconds. The man behind the register put something in a bag (M. couldn't see what it was) and handed it to the girlfriend. The girlfriend thanked him and she and her sister left—the sister turning around one last time to look at M. as she walked out the door.

M. walked back to the shelf and returned the can of green beans to the exact spot he found it. It didn't matter he thought. He had the girlfriend's address scribbled on a piece of paper (in her own handwriting). If she didn't recognize him on a dark night at such a late hour it was understandable. She would recognize him on a bright day at a more reasonable hour and it would be as if they were meeting for the first time all over again—like a second first love but without the burden of love.

He felt awake and excited. Maybe he didn't need a place to sleep, after all. He could stay at the Woodleworth for the night since it didn't close. He would walk from aisle to aisle and read the contents, instructions, or warnings on each can or box or package the shop was selling until morning when he would venture out into the 6 Cities once again. He looked at the shelf and all the cans on the shelf and all the colors and pictures and words on the cans on the shelf and thought that he could look at the cans on the shelf (with all the colors and pictures and words) in the particular order they were in (or in some other order if they were rearranged) and think that they were beautiful. And then he thought that if all the cans (with all the colors and pictures and words) on the shelf were removed and the shelf was completely bare so that the splinters and even the slightest impressions, left behind by the weight of multiple cans stacked on top of each other or just the weight of a single can, were perceptible to the human eye, then he could look at the bare shelf and think that it was beautiful too.

It was a moment like few other moments when he thought that he was very close to finding the answer to why his brother disappeared and didn't return. He felt the mental extract of what he was thinking at that very moment might provide an arrangement for him that he could use to make sense of what happened, what was happening, and what would happen. He would start to understand more while the people who knew him would start to understand him less and think that he was losing his mind when, in fact, or whatever there was of this reality, he was finding it.

He went outside and sat on the ground against the wall beneath the shop window and looked up at the night sky. He saw hundreds of stars and the more his eyes adjusted to the night sky so that he could see hundreds more the less they made sense to him. He felt as if he could reach out to the horizon and pick at the line where the sky met the land and peel it back to reveal the morning before. And if he picked at the morning before he could peel the morning before back to the night before and so on—picking and peeling until he peeled the sky back to the day his brother disappeared.

He would start the morning in the same way (a cup of white rose tea with honey) and carefully repeat everything he had done that day but slow down around noon to make sure that nothing that happened afterwards moved beyond his control so that when the time came in late afternoon (when he saw his brother through the window of his parents' house) he would walk outside, stand beside him—close enough to touch his arm with his own arm—and ask him to please come inside, everyone is waiting for you. But if his brother decided not to come inside then he would leave with him and the taxi driver would still be waiting at the train station or driving someone else around who didn't have a place to stay. Both he and his brother would disappear and the symmetry of their disappearance would provide a small consolation for those who missed them—*those boys are together somewhere, I know it*—whereas the asymmetry of his brother's disappearance alone provided none.

He was close to falling asleep again. The taxi driver walked by him with a bag in her hand and got in the taxi. She beeped the horn. He didn't feel like explaining to her that he was staying at the Woodleworth all night, reading labels on cans and containers, so he got up and walked to the taxi also. As he walked he felt as if he had started to climb. His feet slipped from underneath him and he held on to the edge of the sidewalk outside of the shop, afraid that letting go would plunge him straight to the bottom of the shop and among the assorted goods that had fallen off their shelves and settled there.

He inched his way to the taxi (Jolene heavy on his back), his fingers feeling their way from crease to crease, his feet (his tender foot included) finding ruts on the concrete to push against. He climbed until he reached the taxi and pulled himself inside through the window the taxi driver had opened for him.

His unexpected climbing behavior came from the tremors (perhaps less, vibrations or perhaps even less, sensations—which had taken decades to reach him) that reached him from his tree climbing days when he was a boy. His parents had let his hair and his brother's hair grow long so that when someone walked by the oak tree in front of their house they would look up and see two children climbing the tree, fingers gripped tightly around sturdy branches, one leg stretched to one branch, the other leg stretched to another branch, and yell out some version of the words "you girls be careful up there".

The boys would look down at the passers-by unsure of what they were saying and politely wave but nothing and no one stopped them from climbing higher into the thick middle of the tree where the tree itself became a jungle (blocking out daylight), where no one could see them, and where they might forget that the house they lived in which they could no longer see and seemed hundreds of miles yonder in some unknown direction was simply a pulled branch away from being seen again.

It was in such a place, M. remembered, where he and his brother hid if they didn't want to be found (in the real world) and therefore it made perfect sense to him that it would be in such a place where his brother would hide if he didn't want to be found (in other worlds). M. didn't dream about his brother often (he didn't have to), but he often dreamt about trees, though he couldn't remember climbing one in any dream he ever had.

"I love the Woodleworth", the taxi driver said. "It's my favorite shop in the whole world."

M. wondered whether he should ask the taxi driver about what she bought from the Woodleworth. It didn't seem like a question that someone should mind being asked and was perhaps even desired. Maybe she was ready to open up to him about her purchase(s). But there were considerations beyond the alphabet that formed the words and the words that formed the sentence. What if her answer led him down a path he wasn't prepared for? What if she had bought a hammer (although the bag seemed too big for a hammer—he could see it on the front seat)? Or a syringe?

"Can you take me to the other place?"

"Yes", she said.

They headed towards the bridge that connected the mainland to the small island (streetlights on the opposite side of the river reflected in the water) where the city's most famous landmark—the giant tricycle—had been assembled (in a once-rarely-visited location) by a local sculptor who had attained a small amount of fame (and who had since passed on) for his statue and the scandal that ensued of a woman named Lelolah Vespertina of peculiar shape and prominent marriage before sculpting in obscurity in the hills of the 6 Cities.

During the day little kids played around the giant tricycle although they were too little to climb it. Maybe they had dreams of the giant tricycle later that night or on other restless nights, in which they would suddenly grow to a great height (or perhaps were already grown to a great height), and throw their now-longer leg over the seat of the tricycle, then pedal through the empty roads of the 6 Cities, their heads higher than the buildings (some riding past their own houses or apartments to see—through an opened window—a sister or brother sleeping snugly in bed) before crossing the bridge to the mainland, back-wheels rubbing against the bridge's parapets on both sides, and then off to the flat pastures and grazing lands outside of the city, and then again into the classroom where they learned subtraction or the kitchen where breakfast was always hot and ready whenever they arose. Until then they could play inside the spokes of the giant front wheel while their parents stood around pretending to listen to whatever parents mumble about when they are in each other's company.

It would have been no surprise to anyone if during a conversation fifteen, twenty, thirty, or forty years later that someone who had grown up in the 6 Cities casually remarked among others who had also grown up there that when she or he was younger she or he dreamt about riding the giant tricycle through the city—"me too" one might say while another might confess, in self-deprecating fashion, that she or he still dreamt about the tricycle as an adult.

At night the tricycle belonged to bigger kids who did climb it. And every once in a while it belonged to adults who secretly recalled the mischief they made beneath the tricycle's giant seat whenever they passed by. The taxi driver slowed down around the curve to the bridge and stopped.

"I have nightmares about this bridge", she said.

M. imagined the conversation.

*--But this is a small bridge.*

*--It's not that small.*

*--There's nothing frightening about this bridge.*

*--There is.*

*--I can walk across from here.*

*--It's too cold to walk.*

*--But it's not cold.*

*--It is.*

"I also have nightmares", he said.

He wasn't sure how to respond to the taxi driver but he deduced (in the manner he was taught by Clementine) that she needed reassurance. She slowly drove forward and continued at a slow speed until they were across the bridge. M. had told her the truth although it wasn't what he wanted to tell her. He did have nightmares though the worst dreams he had involved people who were unhappy in real life but happy in his dreams. When he woke up from such dreams the disappointment he felt for those people (and himself) was profound and lasting (for hours and sometimes days). For the taxi driver's part he thought her nightmares consisted of lying on her back in the middle of the bridge, rain pelting her naked body (he had started to take a vague interest in it since he saw her using it out in the open at the Woodleworth), the sound of car and bus engines heaving like a stampede of horses coming around the road, and she unable to move a single muscle while cold drops of rain invaded all the microscopic pores of her skin. Maybe her nightmares consisted of something else. In any case, those were the thoughts that came into his mind.

"Here it is", the taxi driver said. "Don't worry about paying."

He got out of the taxi and closed the door. The taxi driver rolled down the passenger side window.

"Stay warm", she said.

"You too", he said.

She rolled up the window and drove off. M. took a deep breath. He would finally be able to put his head on a soft (but not too soft) pillow, turn on his right side (his favorite sleeping position), and fall asleep. Inside the motel a young woman standing behind the desk welcomed him with a cute smile (causing dimples to appear on her cheeks). The light in the small lobby seemed of this world and the two women who followed him in giggled as they teetered by.

"I'd like a room for the night", he said.

"Of course", the woman said.

He gave her some money and took the key. She pointed the way to the room—up the stairs (where those two are going), second door on the right—and told him that a complimentary breakfast of two croissants and a cup of coffee (unlimited refills until eleven) would be served in the motel's small café beginning at seven o'clock sharp (you won't want to miss it).

He opened the door to his room, finding the light switch with his hand, and flicked it on. But the light was too bright for his eyes and he flicked it off again—there was still enough city light coming through the window to illuminate the bed and the pathway to reach it. He placed Jolene on the floor and lay down.

Whenever he was on the cusp of sleep he turned on his right side. On his back his unwanted memories (his height and weight, the whereabouts of his pencil, or the meaning of a rarely-used word—gynandromorph, for example) cleared themselves out of his head so that only his essential memories stayed behind. It was as if a garden was being weeded so that all that remained (on the surface) was a picturesque geography of flowers—memories that had taken root in the "fertile clay of his mind"—the essence of which seemed to have something in common that he couldn't express outside of his hypnagogic state. And some were in a state of being that he had never encountered outside of that one moment he turned from his back to his right side, as if they weren't flowers at all but pre-flowers of flowers that had yet to grow and that would eventually grow where the darkest flowers grew, in the most melancholy (and rarely-to-never-visited) part of the garden. He could glance at them (a substantial glance) from a distance without ever having to see them up close. The darkest flowers grew apart from the bright flowers (the fragrance of which he could take in all day) and he knew that their roots spread beneath the entire garden, entangling the roots of all flowers (even the brightest) so that uprooting even one of the darkest flowers in the most distant part of the garden would mean uprooting them all.

It was only during that one moment—the turn from his back to his right side (the moment that seemed to last for thirty seconds and sometimes even a whole minute)—that he could take in all the flowers that grew and were about to grow (even visiting the darkest flowers and touching them) in all parts of the garden, when all the flowers, bright and dark, happy and unhappy, revealed something beyond their colors and shapes and bearing—something essential and undeniable.

He heard giggling from another room. The two women who teetered by him in the lobby were talking and as he fell asleep he listened to their conversation as one might listen to a radio. Through the wall their voices sounded soft and beautiful. He wasn't sure he could make out exactly what they were saying but this is what he thought he heard:

"How often do you change your earrings?"

"Two or three times a week."

"I keep them in for the whole week. It's just easier."

"Sometimes I do that too but I get bored with the same ones. What do you want to do tomorrow?"

"Hanami Park."

"We talked about that. You know I don't want go there."

"I know but you'll have to go one day. That's probably why you wanted to come here in the first place. Think about it. We could have gone anywhere."

"No. You wanted to come here. You know I don't want to be anywhere near that place."

"Maybe you want to be near it without being there."

"Maybe. Sometimes I want to be right in the middle of it but I'm afraid. Do you think it's enough to be near it?"

"I don't know."

Hanami Park. "Maybe" that's where he and his new friends (per se) would go to sit (or lie) on the grass and let the day slowly happen. The women stopped talking. He heard a door open in the hallway (the hinges creaked loudly enough to be heard), footsteps (six by the time he started counting), then nothing but his own breathing. The light he saw beneath the door had become impeded by some thing or entity, the shadow of which slunk or tried to slink further beneath the door (taking his breath as its own so that he could only hear the thing or entity breathing while he no longer breathed). A few moments later the shadow disappeared and the light returned. He heard footsteps in the hallway again (nine on second counting) then a door being pulled (the hinges creaked in the same way, albeit of a different tone, on closing) until the recognizable click of the bolt finding its home in the groove of the strike plate.

The women resumed their conversation (they would not be going to Hanami Park the next day) but M. was no longer listening and stared, now disinclined to the world (including the universe) around him, through the opened window at the moon, which was some distance away, but which had started to move nearer and nearer to the window like the illuminated pupil—with the faintest hue of an encircling iris—in the eye of a voyeur (a paramour perhaps peeping through the keyhole of a rival's room) or something (simply the moon) curious to see what was going on between the four walls, ceiling, and floor of his temporary abode.

But it was neither a voyeur nor the moon (although it was the moon) and he saw that it could only be the eye of his brother and nothing else. It was, as is often called something that is without any doubt, unmistakable. And then he remembered the day or that there was a day because he had no idea as to the number that correlated with the day or the name of the day that correlated with the month. He only remembered the month because it was during the very same month that his brother disappeared (how many years ago was it now?—he wanted not to remember but he did) and never returned.

It was as if each month of the year that went by was another turn into focus of a telescope, left behind as a souvenir of the occasion, so that when the day arrived of the so-called anniversary of his brother's disappearance, all the memories and feelings associated with it (the sound of his mother's weeping, the never-before-seen expression on his father's face, the comprehensive destruction of his own heart) were in sharp enough relief to cause further damage to his being (he could think of nothing else to call it)—that part of him (and all other human beings) that could bear so much damage that it seemed inhuman.

He moved to the window. The pupil receded and dimmed, clouds falling over where his brother's other eye (and pupil) should be—like how his brother's hair would fall on one side of his face—with the brightest points of light sparkling through the pores of his skin; a brilliant light that seemed to come from behind the dark wall that was night, until the face that had formed in the night sky faded (into that very same night and perhaps behind it) so that the stars and the moon, which had only recently appeared magnificent to him, suddenly appeared unremarkable compared to the face that he had just seen out there.

Lightning lit up the clouds and he stretched his arm through the window hoping that a wandering discharge would find his hand and give him the power to bring back the dead or find the disappeared (or both). Not far off in the distance he saw the bridge that he had crossed to get there. He saw the taxi—stopped on the approach to the bridge itself—but he couldn't see the driver.

Maybe he could have slept through the night (dreamless) and got up in the morning rested for the day ahead (the address scribbled on the piece of paper came into his mind) but he felt compelled to go "out there". He picked up Jolene and put her on his back, walking (as if he were floating) out into the hallway, down the stairs, through the lobby, placing the key (gently) on the front desk so that it made no noise, and finally through the entrance/exit door of the small motel and once again into the dark night of the 6 Cities. He heard the young woman at the desk calling after him ("you're going to miss breakfast in the morning") but he didn't look back.

It wasn't raining (although it seemed inevitable that one drop of rain from the murky clouds above would spot him and launch itself towards the top of his head—a signal to others that waited impatiently to just "let it all go") but the air around him was steamy so that he perspired around his neck as he walked towards the horizon—the sky above and the earth below, a screen upon which was projected the everyday interactions of familiar (though not cherished) human beings of which he could, in addition to the outward appearance of their bodies, also see the flow of blood through their arteries and veins and the capillaries that connected them; the motion of machines he had used or travelled on top of or inside of (lawn mowers, trains, both electric and non-electric scooters) and their internal mechanisms (if they had such mechanisms); the ferociousness and the gentleness of land, sea, and air animals (none that he had seen in real life)—the blood stained faces of lions at their kill or the river otter carrying her littlest pup to the river bank, a calm wake forming behind her, then dissipating by the time she reaches the shore; and there in the corner of the screen, unnoticed by all whose eyes were drawn elsewhere but not unnoticed by him, a taxi stopped between two streetlamps on the approach to a bridge.

Intermittent light coming from building windows or the occasional passing car made him appear as if he himself were a flickering projection hurrying to make it back onto the screen from where it came before morning and the light that resulted in the fading away of any other projections of light so that no one would (or could) ever know that such a projection (which risked its existence to search other worlds and for which its only substantiation might be the vague impression it made on someone who happened to catch a glimpse of it) had ever been there.

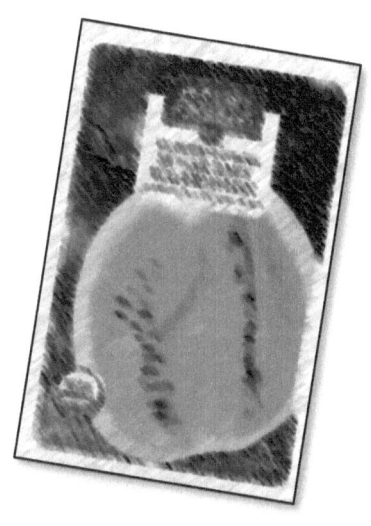

M. was suddenly afraid. Afraid that he was becoming the substance of nightmares (despite—or because of?—his flickering) that cast a darkness on the world around him so that anyone who was his fundamental opposite recoiled at the terror of his being. He felt he could do nothing to stop the darkness he cast unless he also stopped living. He wasn't sure if that's what he was becoming. His brain flickered as well. Maybe it was just how he was feeling at that moment. But it had taken his whole life and everything that he had ever seen and everything that he had ever done or had done to him to feel that way for just that one moment.

As he got nearer to the taxi he saw the taxi driver sitting in the front seat. He tapped on the window as he had done just a few hours before. She didn't look up but he heard the locks of the taxi click open. He got into the back seat. It was as if he had a chance to start again. He had just come off the train, down the stairs, past the vending machine, knocked on the passenger side window of the taxi, heard the taxi driver say "it's cold, get in" (she never said), heard himself ask her where he could stay for the night because he'd never been there before (he remembered saying), heard her say "I know a place" (sounded familiar), and started driving as Jolene leaned into him like a tired friend.

He didn't speak. Instead he thought about the book the young man at the Woodleworth was reading. Or he tried to think about it. He couldn't remember the title. He saw the book cover clearly when he walked into the Woodleworth and he remembered thinking that he had heard of (from Clementine?) or seen (at a bookstore?) that particular book at some point in his life but that he might have been confusing it with the book his brother gave to him and had asked him to read but which he never did.

He tried to picture the scene as he walked into the Woodleworth. Everything in his reimagined image was perfectly clear to him—the sticker stuck to the top of the door handle with the price (1.99) of some petite and most likely discarded plastic object; the balled up chewing gum wrapper on the linoleum floor (well cleaned but dusty after a long day); the two signs for a limited sale on bedding (most likely blankets and pillow cases) hanging (one crooked, one straight) from the ceiling above the breach to the aisle on the far left of the shop; the young man at the register wearing a silver-colored watch on his right hand, a collared (dark blue) shirt with sleeves folded to his elbows; and the book with a blank (light blue) cover that was, without title or artwork (*sans titre ni oeuvre d'art*), impenetrable to any pebble that his memory flung at it. He searched all around him but his memory could find nothing larger to fling. And then in one of those rarest of happenings that never happen to nine-hundred-and-ninety-nine out of one-thousand people in their entire lifetime the taxi driver turned to him and asked: "Did you see the book the man at the Woodleworth was reading?"

"I--", he started saying.

"My Feeling Dress", she said.

He raised his head to see her eyes in the rear-view mirror but she had already turned around to look at him. She was looking at him as she spoke but he was staring at his foot—wondering when it would heal. Her face surprised him. She smiled at him and he smiled back (nervously—his armpits perspired immediately) but he saw nothing happy in her smile. Instead, she looked sadder than ever (than he had ever seen her in the last few hours they were together). To a perceptive watcher of films or studious reader of novels it might have appeared as if she was asking for some kind of recognition of something she didn't want to speak about—perhaps to see if the person in whom she recognized something recognized the same thing in her. But she wasn't asking for anything. She was practicing. And he was no longer concerned about any darkness that he cast. People like her weren't afraid of darkness. Cast it he thought—to keep people who answered questions, who solved problems, who fixed what was broken, away from people like her. He thought maybe he had made her sadder because he didn't notice that she was looking at him when she asked if he saw the book the man at the Woodleworth was reading.

"Have you read it?" she asked.

"No", he said.

But the man at the Woodleworth wasn't reading "My Feeling Dress". He was reading another book (the title of which they would never know) because no one, in the history of writing, including prehistoric times of writing in pictures on cave walls with sharpened rocks or the dynastic-period-of-Egyptian times of writing in hieroglyphics on papyrus with sharpened reeds, had ever written a novel, a story, or poem with the title "My Feeling Dress".

"Maybe one day", she said.

"Maybe one day", he said.

She turned around and pressed on the accelerator. He looked at her eyes in the rear-view mirror as the taxi moved forward. He decided that he wasn't going to ask her where she was taking him. He would just let her take him. It was that time of day he called night-morning (translated as morning-night or day-night in other foreign languages), the time of day he met Clementine (under calamitous circumstances) in the train station, the time of day when it seemed most likely to him that he (and other people) were susceptible to the ways of that all-too-human indulgence called the soul (cumbersome for mingling at parties, talking to neighbors, or watching sporting events) the characteristics of which included—at least in him—a reckless sympathy for the whims and wanderings of people like her.

The realness of their situation at that moment unsettled him. He preferred situations of the imagination: the small garden imagined to be a forest; shopping at the grocery store imagined to be a walk through the boulevards and alleys of a colorful and cosmopolitan city; glances between strangers imagined to be a longing neither would speak about but would think about days, months, or perhaps years later; a silence between passenger and taxi driver imagined to be a conversation between two soon-to-be-lovers who shared revealing stories about their past meanderings through the boulevards and alleys of the colorful and cosmopolitan cities or forests they visited before they met.

He closed his eyes to fall asleep. The sky still threatened rain but not a drop had fallen. Instead, dark grey roses, light grey peonies, the blossoms of a cherry tree of a grey still darker than the roses, a medium-light grey array of carnations, and the black shadows of the darkest grey aster petals broken off from their corolla, drifting in a medium grey ocean of void; and the white moon—glowing just beneath the surface—casting a soft light on all that wandered above and below it.

The taxi driver drove on—past the Tenth Portal (M. opened one eye to see if the light had gone back on in the window near the top of the building—he remembered the woman and man sleeping there), past the train station from where she picked him up, to an apartment building of three stories, four balconies (two with two chairs, one with a bicycle and a chair, one empty), and two patios (one with two chairs and a table, one with three chairs and a broom). She put the taxi in park and turned off the ignition.

"You can stay here for the night", she said.

"What is this place?" he asked.

"I live here", she said. "I don't know where else to take you and I'm very tired. I think you're probably very tired too."

"I am", he said. "But I can sleep in the taxi."

"It's too cold", she said. "You would freeze to death out here. I can take you where you want to go tomorrow."

It was already tomorrow and M. was too tired to imagine the conversation. He reached inside Jolene, got the piece of paper with the girlfriend's address scribbled on it, and gave it to the taxi driver.

"Here is the address", he said.

She took the paper from him and walked ahead carrying the Woodleworth bag with her. He heard the muffled sound of music and saw light and the movement of people in one of the apartment windows on the third floor (the one with the balcony of one chair and a bicycle). She looked at the piece of paper. He heard a bell ring out (four rings). He heard the voices of two men inside a truck passing behind them.

"I know where this is", she said. "It's not very far."

He caught up to her and walked beside her, his hand touching her hand, as his arm moved back and forth, his foot throbbing (a tad) inside his shoe.

"I can carry the bag for you", he said.

"It's okay", she said.

He spied the color (white) of whatever she was carrying in the bag but not the shape or texture. They entered the building and walked up the stairs to the second floor (he fell behind her again). She took a key from her pocket (lifting up her shirt slightly to reveal the soft skin of her lower back) and opened the door to her apartment: a small room with a bed in the middle of the room, a small kitchen, a small bathroom, and a small closet. On a narrow table behind the bed, he saw trinkets (a music box, a small ceramic owl, a miniature plastic horse) that reminded him of the inn where he imagined he and Clementine met as she pulled his foot from the train tracks. On the wall adjacent to the bed he saw photographs of the taxi driver in different places (some he had visited). On a small table in the kitchen, he saw a vase with carelessly arranged flowers (freshly cut) and a single framed photograph of a young woman beside it. He thought that he could rearrange the flowers into the shape of a scalene triangle (as a gift to her for her kindness) if only he had a pair of scissors to cut the stems with. Maybe he could find something sharp in the kitchen (a knife) and do his cutting after she fell asleep.

"I only have one bed", she said. "You can sleep on that side."

She pointed to the right side of the bed. He would be facing her as she slept. Maybe she didn't care. They'd be asleep anyway. But he might stay awake for a little while after she fell asleep and stare at her face (before he searched for something sharp to cut with) to gaze into her soul and find the beauty in her. Because she had some. As much as anyone. And he always wanted to be someone who could find beauty anywhere. If it couldn't be found in the whole song then maybe it could be found in a brief combination of notes or the character of the singer's voice. If it couldn't be found in the whole book then maybe it could be found in a few paragraphs or sentences scattered here and there. If it couldn't be found in the whole body then maybe it could be found in an ear or an elbow.

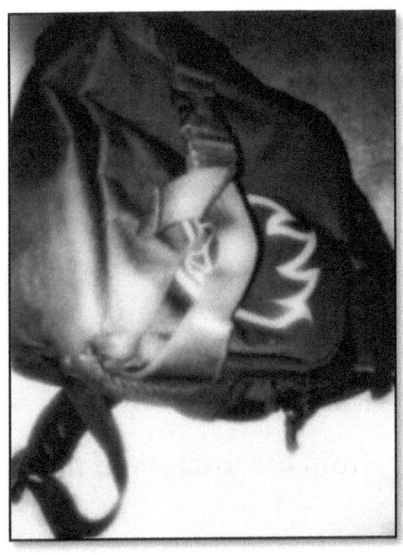

He scanned the room for a book titled "My Feeling Dress" but he saw only magazines. He still had the book his brother had given him to read that he hadn't read yet: *The Unknowed Things*. The author wrote in the short preface at the beginning of the book that he stole the title from his nephew, who himself had written a story called *The Unknown Things* for a school writing assignment. M. would read the book a few years later. His favorite story from the book would be the one titled *the world that destroyed the world.*

---

### *the world that destroyed the world*
### from ***the unknowed things***

The next to last feeling returned. She had somehow become more and together they looked through the telescope to see the outline of the city. They felt there was no hope here. No sun. No rose that burst forth from a moist cloud. No moonlight that shimmered off the gentle waves of the black river drifting before them. This river. From where they were reborn. From where they emerged and stretched out on the land. On the mud. And left the impression of their coil as proof that they once lived. That they once breathed the same air as they who surrounded their outlines with ribbon. As they who visited at night to lay flowers upon the memory of their disappeared forms. As the snakes and toads that swam in the rain-filled cast of their bodies.

Robert says I should know what it is to have been born as another—running through the spray and spittle of gunpowder, hiding beneath the cart of rotting plums and eggplants. All those other, different faces. All unreal to me through the first light of morning. But Martha, I will call her Martha, whispers around his ill-formed ear that only those who made me could have made me and only at that particular moment in history, and that if not then, then never.

I was an uninvited guest to the gathering. An intruder who was available but unprepared for the diversion. The band in the corner beneath the overarching *taxidermia* of the monstrous neck and head of a giraffe, played in tune (or so it was heard) a particular song that brought Robert and Martha to the checkered floor while others watched around them. I sat quietly and thought *do not think for they can find their way in and even now they have already done so. They have schemed within me to give form to their forged existence.*

I asked the trumpeter if I might have a try for I knew a tune that Martha, as a child, played on the rocks and shells she arranged on the footbridge between the road to the beach and her family home. None were allowed to pass until they covered their ears and waited quietly for her to tap her melody with a stick she hid beneath the handrail of the bridge. But it was I who whittled the stick for her and she thanked me by playing her secret melody for me early one morning before our families turned in their beds.

Martha did not look up. But Robert watched me. And I watched him. Over the bell, from where the notes blossomed and then died. Maybe she had tapped this song on the balustrade of the staircase they descended together and told him that no one else in the world had ever heard it. How it must have languished in his ear I thought? Each note knocking the corners of that piece of clumsy furniture protruding from his head.

I watched them above the floor—*the lovers*—lingering in the space the other left behind. I could not deny there was a grace in their movements. As if they were of one form, who only separated for the sake of being understood—an imprecise but charming translation. Martha left the room.

"Ladies and gentlemen," Robert said. "Martha has gone to pee."

There was still something left of her old self after all, I thought. Something for me to hold onto. It wasn't all *balcony above the clouds* and the name of electricity firing through. She had many departures, not the least of which the dress of a kingdom falling upon her body. She sat down: what are we if not living in this world? The face of a boy from which the trench wail and mask. The year in clips of filth. The coat hanging, the severed arms left in curtain sleeves, shoulder blades and neck scraped away. Martha fled and burst around the spiral.

The guests became quiet but it was raining and no one could be certain of what they heard. Paratrooper John came in with a spoon and champagne balloons, kicking his legs up can-can style to the song playing in his head. We only heard his labored breathing, his 'hups' and 'heys' and we clapped awkwardly to his gasping, the hot breath from his nostrils blowing strands of wet hair from his thick moustache onto the floor. The maids came in and swept up the mess. And then he clenched a fist, raised his arm, and yelled "The war is over! Hooray!", until he noticed a *moustachito*, black and gleaming, on the floor beneath him.

I accidentally punctured the wall behind me. When I turned around Robert was looking through the window. Beyond him I saw the outline of the city. The rain flowed along the rooftops and spires and surged like a waterfall over the edge of the last building (the truest building), and cascaded down his arm, dripping from the fingers of his hand.

Old Bobby knew the absence would irk me and when he walked away there was so much space beside the city that I fell into a panic. I thought I saw Martha out there in a tungsten ploddy rowing herself to death but she was peeing, although the sound of her peeing was drowned out by drops of rain hitting the oversized pancreatic kettle the gardener kept out back. Robert knocked on the bathroom door but Martha did not answer and when he burst in we saw the open window. Oh the breeze. It blew the curtain out and in and enveloped us with a feeling that most resembled freedom. No one spoke though everyone had ideas about what had happened. I saw them (snarl) just above their heads in perfect spheres that rose up like bubbles and burst upon the ceiling.

They continued their dance and I asked Robert if I might cut in. He nodded and I put my arm around Martha's waist and pulled her close to me. This was *my* Martha. I moved her hair away from her face and pressed my cheek to hers. I watched the back of Robert's head as he walked away, and that ear, the shape of D'Artagnan the elder→hackmate of his Prostruscan master→martyred for a commonly known descriptive phylum→unable to dodge the laments and hoarse cries of *laud me but make no mention*—that ear I could take an ax-mop to, to chop and then mop pieces of into a dust bin and pour into a fire to warm anywhere it was too cold to sleep. The building shook. Robert had climbed the giraffe and straddled the neck like he was hunter Sally.

Meanwhile, my shoulders twitched uncontrollably. I knew the song. It was from our later years and Martha and I moved in perfect accord. As her breasts plunged in, my chest became concave. As my hip thrust forward, her atoms tingled around the striations of my thigh. She followed me as I pulled her here and there. Back across the river to the 6 Cities and cans of mixed vegetables (golden carrots, golden corn, and golden peas), medium-sized golden chicken eggs and golden-golden dirigibles. I winked for a tango but the music ended and Martha bowed her head to thank me because she could see that I knew how to boogie. And yet, not a hint of recognition. Not a twinkle in her eye that she had tried to access the deep well of her brain matter to pull me out and bring me front and center. Oh Martha, what is that you cannot see? Someone yelled "yeeeeehah!". I heard a bone snap and felt a wobble around my titular array.

When we lived in this place, I held the (blaise) omnibus of her flower.

*--the end--*

The taxi driver reached into the Woodleworth bag and pulled out a soft, white blanket. She unfolded the blanket and placed it on top of the blanket already on her bed, walking around the bed to pull each corner of the blanket to make sure the blanket (and the mattress) underneath was entirely covered. She took off her shirt and pants (in that order), threw them onto the floor (pants on top of shirt), and gently got underneath both blankets. She turned onto her right side, away from M. (he wouldn't be able to gaze into her soul, after all—the four words swirled in his brain like lost electrons attaching themselves to his thoughts as if the four words and his thoughts were incomplete without each other: it wasn't a cold gaze into her soul day today, I'll see the girlfriend gaze into her soul tomorrow, her gaze into her empty soul and lonely balcony, etc. etc.—for what better reason was there to stare at the face of another human being?).

He placed Jolene at the foot of the bed and lay on his back (on top of both blankets), eyes opened, looking up at the ceiling. As he started to fall asleep and before he turned on his right side he felt as if he were floating on a tranquil body of water, a slow-moving river, he moving even slower than the river, looking up at a sky he had not seen since his brother disappeared, a bright and orderly affair (unlike the disorganized and uncertain sky of the possible-clouds and sometimes-rain that hung over him) annotated with a sweet breeze that drifted across his face and the parts of his body—his feet, his knees, his arms—uncovered by the river and brought to life by the convergence of the natural elements in that open air around him but perceived from afar, perhaps by children playing on a nearby hill, as pieces of rotting wood drifting aimlessly along; a sky in which the sun and moon moved back and forth across a genteel and languid expanse like two beads on the invisible rod of a giant abacus, each used in turn to count the days and nights of a happy if not meaningful life in a world (including the universe) in which such days could be counted up to a tidy sum, placed into a small sack like pieces of gold, and then buried for all time. His days, on the other (or either) hand, seemed uncountable.

He turned onto his right side and accidentally pushed Jolene off the bed. He had forgotten to close her and, as she tumbled over and upside down, everything that she carried inside her fell out and onto the floor below: a pencil, a notepad, a wooden butter knife (stolen from the inn but never used), two paper hearts (he and Clementine made at the Chinese diner), a fishing lure (never used), the book *The Unknowed Things* given to him by his brother (never read), one packet of white rose tea, one packet of watermelon seeds, his brother's hat, and an old photograph of his brother he had taken from his parents' house. After he fell asleep, the sound of his brother's voice woke him, and he stood up on the river, looking at all the trees around him. It would be in the trees where he would find what he was looking for, where he could embrace the world (including the universe) and be free from it at the same time.

AR

www.ingramcontent.com/pod-product-compliance
Lightning Source LLC
Chambersburg PA
CBHW030906170426
43193CB00009BA/757